AMERICAN NEON

AMERICAN NEON

Compiled by Kathy Mack

Universe Books

New York

Published in the United States of America in 1976
by Universe Books
381 Park Avenue South, New York, N.Y. 10016

Library of Congress Catalog Card Number: 76-15043

Cloth edition: ISBN 0-87663-276-2
Paperback edition: ISBN 0-87663-950-3

Printed in the United States of America

INTRODUCTION

Since the 1920s, neon signs have permeated the American landscape: from Times Square in New York to Santa Fe, New Mexico, neon has been the object of attention and criticism. Yet most Americans know very little about the origins or technique of neon signmaking; it is, in fact, confused with electric signage. And few are aware that neon signs are individually produced, handmade works.

Sir William Ramsay, an English chemist, discovered neon in 1898 while he was investigating the composition of liquid air. Neon is a chemically inert, colorless gas, which turns reddish-orange when it is inserted into vacuum tubular lamps through which an electric current is passed.

In 1910, Georges Claude demonstrated the first commercial neon sign at the Grand Palais in Paris. The following year, the first neon sign in the United States was erected by a Los Angeles car dealer. People were so fascinated by the glowing sign that they drove for miles to see it. By the mid-1920s, neon was being produced in the U.S. under the Claude patent, and "Claude Neon" was such a common expression that it was widely believed that the founder of the industry was a Mr. Claude Neon.

Even though neon was more expensive than electric signage, advertisers were immediately receptive to it, for several reasons. The color of the light, while easy on the eye, is extremely compelling. Because of the versatility of its tubing, neon is highly flexible for creating difficult designs and unique patterns. The vast color range of neon tubing ranges from intense reds to soothing pastels. Under normal conditions, neon is easy to maintain and has a long life.

Within a short time, neon was adapted to all types of indoor and outdoor business advertising, and neon companies were overwhelmed with orders. Signs were erected in most major American cities, beginning in New York and Los Angeles and spreading throughout the country. The neon sign business continued to grow, flourishing during the business boom of 1925-29, and peaking after World War II. At that time, there were more than 3,500 neon sign men in the United States; now there are fewer than 250.

After its boom in the late 1940s, the use of commercial neon began a slow but steady decline. General Electric introduced electric signs that could be mass produced centrally and were, therefore, cheaper. Many companies found neon maintenance costly and difficult, since outdoor signs could be damaged by heavy windstorms or hurled rocks. The glass tubing companies discontinued many of the more obscure tubing colors, and neon blowers became a dying breed since there had been no formal apprenticeship in their craft. Zoning laws promoted by environmentalists outlawed certain types of signs in many areas, including New York City.

The energy crisis of the early 1970s dealt the most drastic blow to the neon sign business: signs were turned off in order to conserve energy, even though neon uses very little electricity. Many were never again turned on; others needed costly repairs in order to operate again. Consequently, neon went the way of countless other crafts: it was swallowed up by mass production and big business.

Neon sculpture, however, has grown considerably within the last ten years, and classes in neon production are now taught at some colleges and art schools. Galleries and museums have exhibited neon sculpture, and artists such as Chryssa, Antonakos, and Billy Apple have gained prominence in the medium. There is a resurgence in the use of neon as an integral architectural light source, and individuals have begun collecting both old and new neon.

The word "neon" is generally used to describe glass tubing of all colors, but the term is misleading since neon gas produces only the most popular reddish-orange color. Various rare gases produce a variety of other colors, and a phosphorous coating on the inside lining of a tube can expand the color range even more. Another basic gas, argon, is ultraviolet; argon combined with mercury yields a blue sign; the same gases in a yellow rather than a clear tube produce green. Helium is white-gold; xenon is blue-white; krypton combined with argon is purple.

All neon signs are handmade. The first step in their construction is the preparation of an asbestos pattern drawn to scale. Sections of tubing are heated over a low flame; as the glass softens, it is bent to conform to the pattern. Electrodes are then melted onto the tubing in a similar manner, one at each end. After the design is completed and the electrodes joined, the existing air is removed from the tubes. The signmaker then introduces the gas into the tube through a rubber hose, filling it to a specific pressure. The tubing is then sealed off and all connecting tubes are blacked out by tape or paint. The sign is then ready to be mounted and connected to a transformer which provides the necessary electricity. The sign is now completed and may be plugged in for use.

The photographs in this book illustrate only a small percentage of the neon signs in use in the United States today. The days of neon's prominence are probably gone forever, but now neon can be appreciated for what it is: a handmade art, a symbol of Americana, and a joy to behold.

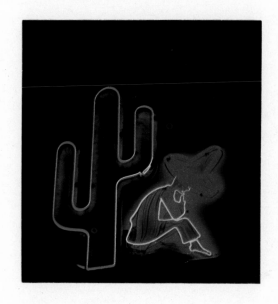

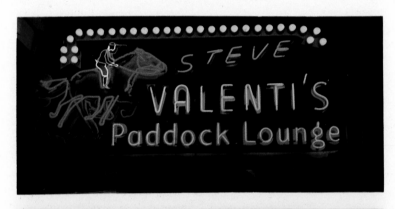

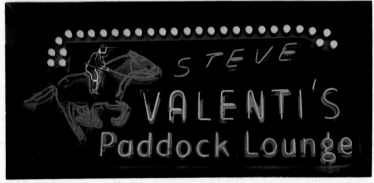

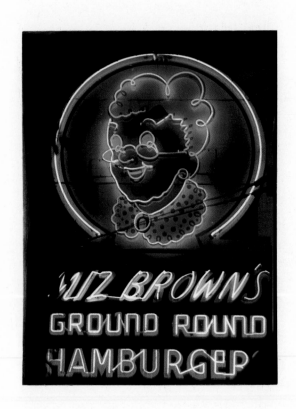

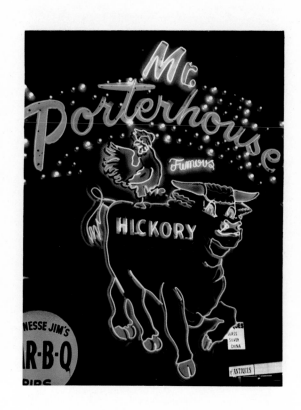

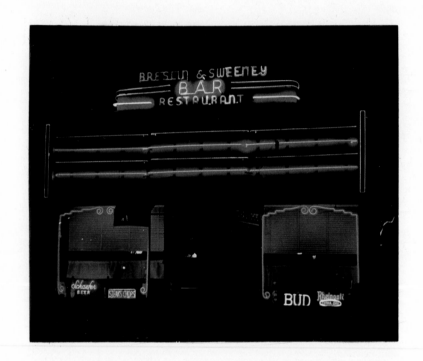

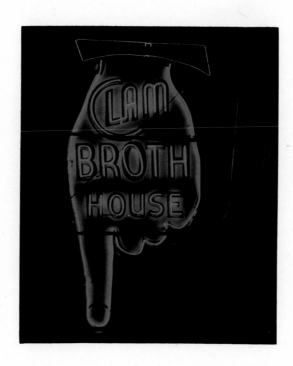

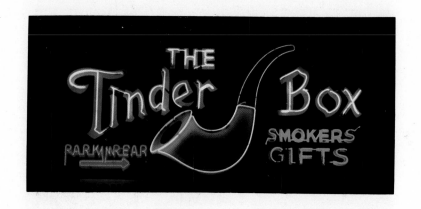

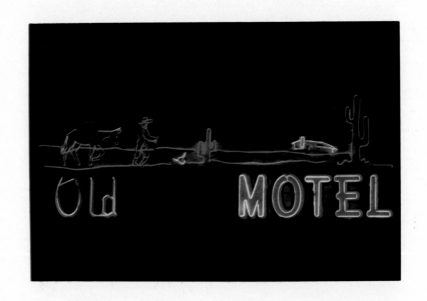

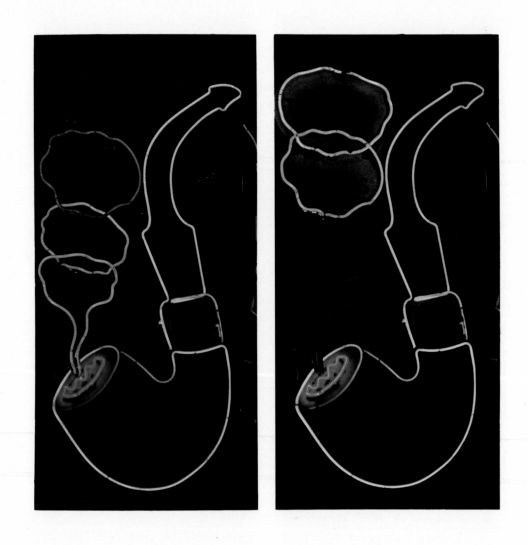

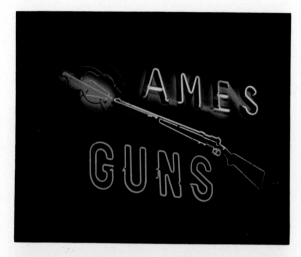

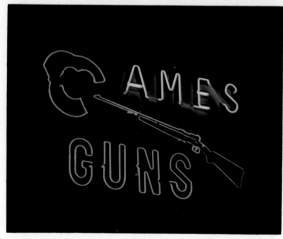

45

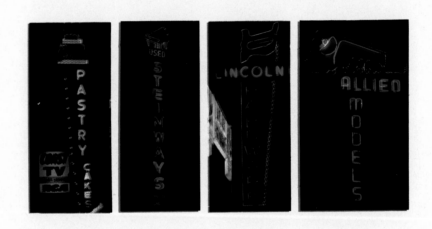

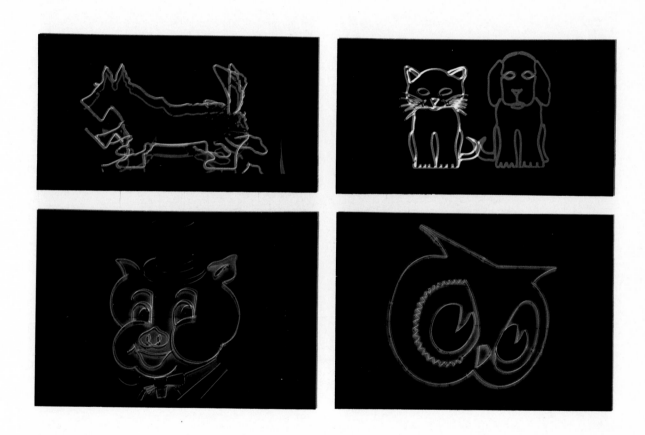

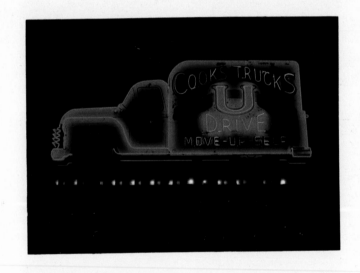

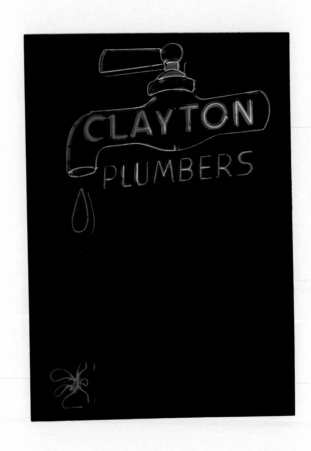

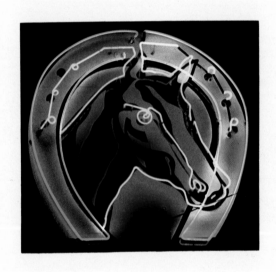

69

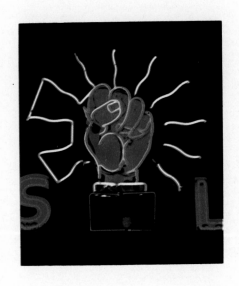

70

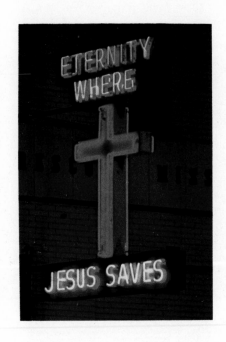

LIST OF ILLUSTRATIONS

CREDITS

Photographs

James Mack: 14, 17, 20, 22, 23, 25-27, 30-33, 38, 41-43, 46, 48, 49, 51-53,
                55 (top left), 56, 58, 61, 68, 69, 72.
Kathy Mack: 3-7, 11-13, 16, 18, 19, 28, 34, 35, 36, 39, 40, 47, 59, 63-66, 70.
Moya Studio, Chicago: 2.
Kathy Rosenbloom: 1, 9, 39, 55 (top right).
Gerry Stableski: 8, 10, 21, 24, 29, 35, 44, 45, 50, 55 (lower left, lower right),
                54, 57, 60-62, 67.

Cover

Sign designed by Joe Duffy
Sign made by Nordquist Sign Co., Minneapolis
Sign photographed by John Ligon
Design by Robert Reed

ACKNOWLEDGMENTS

I wish to thank the following people
for their support and assistance:
Kathy Rosenbloom, who gave hours of time on this project;
Rich Dolack; Chuck Dorsey; Joe Engelberg of Glo-Tube;
John and Margi Ligon; Cork Marcheschi; Mr. and Mrs. Melvin Mack; Jim Mack;
Jerry Palubniak; Mr. Miles Pennybacker; Al Slarks of Nordquist Sign Co.;
Jeannie Trusty Stiles; David Strout of Hallmark Cards;
Mitzi Tessler; Carmine Tosta of Midtown Neon Sign Corp.;
Michael Tuttle; Bill Crosby and Craig Reynolds of Voltarc Tube Company;
Wells Wright of Naegele Outdoor Advertising;
and one other who shall remain nameless
but whose support was and is essential.